JOSHUA RASMUSSEN, PH.D.

THE
BRIDGE
OF
REASON

TEN STEPS TO SEE GOD

PUBLISHED BY

G

Great Legacy Books

 Great Legacy Books
www.greatlegacybooks.com

The Bridge of Reason: Ten Steps to See God
Copyright © 2018 by Joshua L. Rasmussen

All rights reserved.

No part of this book may be used or reproduced in any manner whatsoever without written permission except in the case of brief quotations embodied in critical articles or reviews. For permissions, contact sales@greatlegacybooks.com.

For more resources from the author, visit his website:
Joshua L. Rasmussen
www.joshualrasmussen.com

Cover design and interior layout by Rachel M. Rasmussen.
Cover image compliments of Pixabay.
www.pixabay.com

ISBN: 978-1-7323834-3-2

First Edition
10 9 8 7 6 5 4 3 2 1

Printed in the United States of America.

CONTENTS

INTRODUCTION 3
STEP ONE -EXISTENCE- 9
STEP TWO -PUZZLE- 17
STEP THREE -FOUNDATION- 17
STEP FOUR -ETERNAL- 25
STEP FIVE -PURELY ACTUAL- 35
STEP SIX -FOUNDATION OF MIND- 41
STEP SEVEN -FOUNDATION OF MATTER- 51
STEP EIGHT -FOUNDATION OF MORALS- 57
STEP NINE -FOUNDATION OF MATH- 69
STEP TEN -THE GREATEST TREASURE- .. 77
NEXT STEPS 89
ABOUT THE AUTHOR 95

INTRODUCTION

Does *blind faith* concern you? Does it bother you when people believe in things without any objective reasons or evidence?

Maybe you were once part of a group of "believers," or you know people who are part of such a group. Or maybe you believe in God, or would like to believe, but you have doubts. You see many people appealing to emotions and values rather than to evidence. When they *do* cite evidence, it often feels like they are under the blanket of confirmation bias. Perhaps you wonder whether these people truly want the truth. Would they follow the evidence if it contradicted their pre-existing viewpoint?

If you can relate to these concerns, this book is for you. The questions you ask are the mark of an explorer. They take courage to ask. When you face reality honestly, you risk discovering things you don't like. You risk breaking your hopes and expectations. Perhaps that has happened to you many times already.

Despite the risks, there is a great reward for facing reality for what it is. That reward is freedom. Freedom to see things for yourself. Freedom to increase your understanding of the real world. Freedom to design your life in accordance with the systems and rules that actually exist.

The purpose of this book is to provide a *bridge of reason* that leads to a universal treasure. While it takes courage to seek truth, it also takes courage to search for a treasure. This book is about the intersection between truth and treasure.

This book is not a post-hoc rationalization of a religion. It is not about defending a tribe or ideology. Many books on "apologetics"—i.e., defenses of a worldview—seek to reinforce a tribe. That's not my goal. I am an explorer, a philosopher who seeks to uncover universal truths that can serve others.

You may be skeptical. That's good. Skepticism protects you from error. I invite you, therefore, to test everything I say with the instrument of your own reflection. As I lay out the steps, I will use planks of rational thought and universal experience. Those are my building blocks. I will build this bridge one step at a time.

The bridge of reason is yours to own, to assess, and to build upon. I offer it humbly as a gift for your consideration.

Enjoy the journey.

STEP ONE
-EXISTENCE-

The first step onto the bridge is about something everyone from all cultures at all times experiences: *existence*. For example, you experience the existence of your own body. You experience the existence of your thoughts, feelings, and desires. The experience of existence is universal.

I don't mean anything fancy by the term "existence." I just mean that *there are* things. There are houses. There are rocks. There are people. *You* are among the things there are.

You might wonder whether everything could just be an illusion. Perhaps we live in the Matrix, where machines trick us into believing in a real world. Perhaps instead of seeing actual trees, we only "see" our *experience of trees*. In that case, all our experiences are part of an elaborate deception. Nothing is as it seems.

But even if everything is an illusion, the *illusion* exists! If we are in the Matrix, the Matrix exists.

I do not claim that everything is as it seems. The first step onto the bridge is to see merely that *something* exists, whatever it might be.

Suppose you deny that anything exists. Then your *denial* exists. To deny the existence of everything implies the existence of something. Although something, like you, *could* deny that there is something, doing so is self-defeating. It is self-defeating for something to deny the existence of everything.

To be clear, maybe you are radically different in nature than you think. Maybe you are a brain in a vat. It does not matter. You can still step onto the bridge of reason.

At this point, you might think it is obvious enough that at least *something* exists. You might even wonder why I am starting with something so obvious. Certainly, I don't wish to insult your intelligence.

I have a simple reason for starting with something obvious: I want our steps to be secure. I do not want to appeal to guessing. I don't want to appeal to blind faith. I want each step to be *knowable*.

Before I continue, I want to point out two things that are *not obvious* about the obvious. Understanding these things will help motivate our journey. First, *obvious* truths are not the same as *trivial* truths. For example, while it may be obvious that you exist, your existence is far from trivial. (We will come back to the significance of your existence later in the book.)

Similarly, consider the axioms of mathematics. They are obvious enough. But they are not trivial. They are the foundation for countless theorems and technologies.

Moreover, and to the point, while it is obvious that *something exists*, this obvious starting point is not trivial, as we shall see. If you think about existence in a still, quiet moment, its significance can startle you.

Here is a second thing that's easy to miss about the obvious. What can be obvious *to you* is not automatically obvious to everyone else; and what can be obvious *to me* is not automatically obvious *to you*. Have you ever been in a conversation with someone who disagreed with you about something you think—you *know*—is true? Why the disconnect? In my experience as a philosopher, I have discovered that everything—and I mean *everything*—can be doubted. Even the existence of all doubts can be doubted. I'm not saying it's reasonable to doubt everything. I'm saying it's possible.

Reason is a light, but it doesn't force sight on anyone. Whatever can be *known* can be *occluded*. Whatever can be *seen* can be *invisible*. Whatever can be *discovered* can remain *hidden*.

Even if many people know a thing, others can fail to know it. Not everything that *can* become clear to you *must* be perfectly clear to everyone at every time. Obstacles can block sight.

I mention the possibility of not seeing the obvious because I want to help you avoid a certain barrier to sight. That barrier is composed of the voices of people who *do not see*. When scientists began to discover that the earth is not the center of the solar system, they saw something. Yet many people voiced opposition to what they saw. Science skeptics didn't see what the scientists saw. That didn't mean that the scientists didn't actually have sight, or that others couldn't come to have more sight.

It takes courage to be a skeptic, yet it also takes courage to strain to see what others do not (yet) see.

Maybe you doubt that certain things can be seen. There are some things you do not see, and maybe you don't see how anyone *could* see those things. That's understandable. It's reasonable. In fact, that's exactly why I am drawing attention to the possibility of not seeing something that can be seen. I wish to inspire within your mind the idea that there is still more to be seen, more than anyone has yet seen. More sight is always possible.

In the steps to follow, I will shine the light of reason on things I think you *can* see. I think you can see these things because I think I see them. Ultimately, of course, you will be the judge of what you think you can see. If there is an obstacle standing in the way of sight, I want to help you remove it, if I can.

STEP TWO
-PUZZLE-

So far, we have seen that *something exists*. The existence of something leads to a puzzle, however. Our second step is to see that puzzle.

The puzzle arises when we consider a simple question: why is there *anything*? Why not instead nothing?

We can imagine a world without anything in it. Imagine no stars, no planets, no particles, anywhere, ever. Just blank. Even if we cannot visualize completely empty space, we can still grasp the idea of completely empty space. Space could conceivably be empty. Why isn't it? Why are all these atoms moving around? Why is there *us*? Why not instead just blank, empty space, forever?

Perhaps you have pondered this question before. What may be hard to see, however, is why this question is so puzzling. You might think the answer to the question is simple: *nothing explains existence*, and that's that.

Yet, there is more to the puzzle. The puzzle I have in mind is composed of two parts. The first part is revealed by reason. The second is suggested by experience. Together they reveal a paradox.

Start with the first part. Reason reveals something about existence in total. It reveals that *nothing beyond existence created existence*. Let me be clear about what I mean. I am talking about a producer that stands outside all of existence. Nothing that *exists* stands outside all of existence. Hence, nothing that exists produced all of existence. Thus, we have the following principle about existence:

> *Principle of Uncaused Existence: nothing created existence.*

If something created existence, then this something would exist just prior to the creation of existence. That means prior to existence, it would both exist and not exist—which is a contradiction.

So far so good: this result confirms that existence in total was not created. However, a paradox arises when we reflect on our universal experience of *creation*. Everything we experience has a creation—i.e., something caused or produced it. The words on this page, for example, didn't magically appear from nowhere. They came from my mind, which in turn came from prior states of reality. Similarly, when a tree falls, wind and gravity work to create its fall. Flowers form from seeds. Seeds form from previous flowers. Cars move by engines inside. In fact, everything you do and see comes from prior states. Everything is part of a *causal order*. In other words, it would seem that universal experience reveals the following principle:

Principle of Caused Existence: all existence is created.

But now we have a paradox on our hands. The Principle of Uncaused Existence reveals that existence itself is *not created*. Yet, by observation, every instance of existence is *created*. How is that possible?

Here is an idea: the *"whole show"*—existence in total—is different from things *inside* the show. Maybe everything *in* existence was created, while existence itself was not.

This idea is in the right direction. But it is incomplete. It doesn't yet explain *why* or *how* the whole show can exist. Consider that the *wholes* we experience have outside causes. For example, both your computer (the whole thing) and its parts are the products of creation. Similarly, a movie has actors and props that have causes. But so does the whole movie. Both the show and its parts are the products of creation.

Notice that *size* makes no difference. Legos and galaxies alike come from somewhere. Small things and big things are products of creation. It is no easier for a turtle to snap into being from nothing than for a stack of infinitely many turtles.

To draw out this point, imagine a scenario where an infinite stack of turtles upon turtles comes into existence. We can describe the scenario like this. Turtle 1 is produced at 5 pm by turtle 2. Turtle 2 is produced by turtle 3 at 4:30 pm. Turtle 3 is produced by turtle 4 at 4:15 pm. In general, each earlier turtle is produced in *half* the time as the next. By this procedure, it turns out that an *infinite* series of turtle creations occurs between 4 pm and 5 pm. In other words, an infinite number of turtles will have been produced, each by another turtle, within one hour. This scenario may be conceivable (in some sense). But it contradicts all experience. No stack of interdependent turtles—of any number—ever emerges *from nothing*—no matter the place or time.

It makes no difference if we extend the *length of time*. We can imagine an eternal turtle, but eternal age does nothing to make such a turtle *actual*. An eternal turtle may be conceivable (in some sense). But conceivability is not enough to explain *actual existence*.

In view of these considerations, it is tempting to think that the Principle of Caused Existence is general: *everything*, of any size, is created by something. Yet, that contradicts the Principle of Uncaused Existence: existence in total is uncreated. Nothing stands outside existence in total. Thus, we have a paradox.

STEP THREE
-FOUNDATION-

Here is where we are so far: something exists. The existence of something, whatever it is, inspires a question: *why*? Why does *anything* exist? This question leads to the puzzle of *uncaused existence*. Existence in total is like a giant castle. Everything in the castle, including smaller castles, are the products of creation. Yet the giant castle, in total, is not the product of creation. How can that be?

Reflection on this question is a key to unlock treasures of insight.

In graduate school, while at the University of Notre Dame, I read over a hundred books and articles on this topic. Since then, I have had more than a thousand conversations about the origin of reality with people of all sorts. In my studies, I have found an answer—an ancient answer—that has stood the test of time, and incredibly, it stands the test of conversations with many minds.

You might wonder how I can be so bold. How can I say that I have *the answer*? Well, it would be dishonest of me to pretend I don't see something that I think I do see. You will be the judge.

As you consider what I am about to share, you might be reminded of similar ideas you have heard before. Follow me carefully. Do not let similar ideas distract you. I have sorted through many nearby ideas that flicker like embers. They are not the flame. The path I am constructing is precise. It takes us through a very specific set of ideas. In order for our steps to be secure, we will need to step along a precise path.

I will now reveal the solution to the puzzle of uncaused existence. The reason the "giant castle" (the totality of existence) has no cause of its existence is that it contains a *fundamental layer*. This fundamental layer is a unique kind of reality. It has a nature that precludes its own creation. It is the sort of thing (whether one or many) that exists uncaused, uncreated, and unproduced. I shall call this foundational layer, "the foundation."

The foundation is unlike a turtle. A turtle can have causes that created it. In fact, a turtle *must* have some creation if it is to exist. The foundation is different. It cannot have a creation. Its nature precludes it.

We will dig deeper into what sort of nature could preclude its own creation. But here I want to make sure we are not proceeding too quickly. I have proposed that each step on our bridge is knowable. Hence, I want to make it clear why I say this third step—the step to a foundation—is knowable.

How can we know that existence requires a foundation? Here is how. Take any bit of *created* reality, a grain of sand, say. When I say this grain is created, I mean some prior thing or things caused it to exist. I leave open *how* it was created. Maybe it was produced by certain atoms, as they came together to form a grain of sand. The details don't matter. What matters is that this grain of sand was created *somehow*.

Next, observe that *combining* grains of sand also yields a created reality. A pile of sand, just like a grain of sand, is a created reality. Similarly, a stack of turtles is a created reality; no stack of turtles appears from nowhere. These observations are part of a universal observation: created realities add to form *created* realities.

Suppose we say instead that created realities could add up to an uncreated reality. Then we have a construction error. Just as *white marble* tiles cannot add to form a *black, non-marble* floor, purely dependent, created things cannot add to form a non-dependent, non-created "castle."

Reason itself reveals the construction error. By reason, you can see that dependence cannot add up to independence. From dependence comes only dependence. From created parts come a created whole.

We are not committing a "fallacy of composition" here. The opposite is so: we are avoiding a construction error—a construction *fallacy*. Just as white marble tiles cannot add up to a steel black floor, dependent tiles cannot add up to an independent floor. If a castle is composed of purely dependent, created blocks, then the whole castle must be dependent and created, by its nature.

Notice that differences in time and place make no difference. It is no easier for created stones to form an uncreated castle in North Dakota than in New Jersey. Similarly, it is no easier for a castle to be uncreated today than yesterday. Differences in location or time are completely irrelevant.

We are now prepared to solve the paradox we encountered earlier. Recall the paradox: the Principle of Caused Existence contradicts the Principle of Uncaused Existence. Hence, they cannot both be true. We can be sure that the Principle of Uncaused Existence is true, since we can be sure that nothing stands (*exists*) outside all existence. That much is clear. The problem, then, *must* be with the Principle of Caused Existence. The Principle of Caused Existence is close to truth. That's why it is tempting to believe it. Yet, reason sharpens our sight. It's not true that *everything* is created. Rather, it's true that everything with a *dependent nature* is created. Thus, we have the following principle:

> *Principle of Dependence: purely dependent things form dependent totals.*

This principle has two witnesses: universal experience and

reason. By universal experience, we witness dependent things forming dependent totals. We never witness an exception. Moreover, reason confirms this result. By reason, dependence cannot add up to independence.

We now have the pieces for securing our third step. The "big castle," which includes all of existence, is uncreated. Yet, by the Principle of Dependence, every composition of purely dependent things is created. Therefore, the "big castle" is not a composition of purely dependent things. Instead, the uncreated "castle" has an uncreated *foundation*. This foundation, unlike created, dependent things, is uncreated and independent.

The next step is to have a closer look at the nature of the foundation.

STEP FOUR
-ETERNAL-

T he steps so far take us to the foundation of reality. This foundation is like the floor of a large castle. Without the floor, there would be no castle. Without the foundation, there would be no reality.

We will now use the light of reason to begin to investigate this foundation. What is the foundation's nature?

To help us think about this question, imagine you have some Play-Doh. This Play-Doh, let's say, represents the foundation of everything. It is the uncreated source of everything else. It is uncreated because it is the foundation of all creation.

What kind of a thing can be uncreated? To help us think about this question, let us start with an example of something that is created. Imagine forming the Play-Doh into a Gumby figure. This Gumby figure does not appear from nothing. Unless something creates a Gumby figure, there will *never* be a Gumby figure. A Gumby figure remains a merely *potential* reality until it is created. In general, a merely potential reality is never actual unless something makes it actual.

The foundation, by contrast, is different. The foundation—*by definition*—is *not* created. Hence, it is not a merely potential reality. Instead, it is *automatically actual*.

How can something be automatically actual? Think again about the Play-Doh. It represents the uncreated foundation. That means this Play-Doh, we are supposing, has never been a *mere potential*, like Gumby. That's the key. The kind of thing that can be uncreated is precisely the kind of thing that cannot be a mere potential. Let me say this again:

> *The kind of thing that can be uncreated is precisely the kind of thing that cannot be a mere potential.*

Suppose instead the uncreated foundation could be a mere potential. Then it could be created. Yet, to be created is against its nature. It has a nature that precludes creation. Therefore, the uncreated foundation has a nature that precludes *mere potentiality*. The foundation cannot be a mere potential.

These concepts are not easy, and as I mentioned earlier, there are neighboring ideas that can easily distract our attention. Thus, for the sake of increasing clarity, I want to have a closer look at the concepts in play.

Consider what it means for a foundation to be a *foundation*. To be a foundation is to be uncreated. To be uncreated is to be *independent.* That is to say, the foundation doesn't depend on anything else for its existence. Instead, it is *self-sufficient.*

Whatever is self-sufficient cannot be a *mere potential.* For a mere potential is just the sort of thing that *can be created.* Yet, a self-sufficient foundation *cannot be created.* Thus, we have the following principle about self-sufficiency:

> *Principle of Self-Sufficiency: whatever has a self-sufficient nature has a necessary nature (i.e., no potential for non-existence).*

Both reason and universal experience testify to this principle. By reason, we see that a mere potential, like a Gumby figure, cannot be actual without any cause or explanation. Universal experience confirms this: we never witness mere potentials become actual from nothing.

The Principle of Self-Sufficiency sheds light on the foundation of reality. The foundation is self-sufficient. So, by the Principle of Self-Sufficiency, the foundation has a necessary nature (i.e., no potential to not be actual). It follows that the foundation cannot be created or destroyed.

At this point, you may have a few questions. I will address three questions that commonly come up.

First, you might wonder whether this foundation could be *matter* or *energy.* After all, energy cannot be created or destroyed. It just changes forms, like Play-Doh. Perhaps, then, the foundation of existence is merely material.

My answer is that, as far we have seen so far, material stuff is indeed an excellent candidate for being the foundation. I have said nothing (yet) to rule that out. In fact, for those who think matter is all there is, the hypothesis that matter is the foundation is useful. It can help you remove obstacles to the steps we have seen so far. It can give you a framework for *conceiving* of a foundation that cannot be created or destroyed. As far as we have seen so far, maybe the foundation is entirely material.

On later steps, I will draw attention to something that is more fundamental than matter. There I will explain why matter—as it is normally conceived, anyway—cannot be the basic layer of reality. But let us not get ahead of ourselves. At this point, the steps take us merely to an automatically actual foundation.

A second question that people sometimes bring up is about *virtual particles*. They point out that, according to current science, virtual particles are able to appear spontaneously from nothing. Hence, perhaps the foundation of existence appeared from nothing, like a giant virtual particle. Why not?

Here is why. Science reveals—at most—that virtual particles appear *spontaneously* or *indeterminstically*. To illustrate, consider your own (apparent) ability to act spontaneously. For example, you can spontaneously start waving your arm. To be clear, spontaneous waving is not the same as completely uncaused waving. On the contrary, if you

Step Four: Eternal

wave your arm, then *you* (or your intentions) are the cause. Just because you didn't *have to cause* your arm to wave (i.e., it was spontaneous) doesn't mean you didn't *actually cause* it to wave.

Similarly, a particle might spontaneously emerge, but that doesn't mean the particle emerged from nothing. Just because the universe didn't *have to cause* the particle (i.e., it was spontaneous) doesn't mean it didn't *actually cause* it to exist. On the contrary, virtual particles emerge from prior states of energy. They come from something. This result matches both universal experience and reason.

Finally, you might wonder about the first event of the universe (if there is a first event). Maybe the first event, unlike all others, is the one event that can appear uncaused. Maybe something can come from nothing *just one time*. Why couldn't that be?

Although the answer may not be initially obvious, we can discover the answer by paying close attention to the *nature of differences in time*. Let me explain. Differences in time are differences in *when* events happen, not *whether* events can be uncaused. Is a giant castle more able to appear from nothing on Tuesday than on Wednesday? Clearly not. Reason reveals why: the difference between Tuesday and Wednesday is not relevant to a castle's ability to appear from nothing. Differences in time are irrelevant. All times are intrinsically alike, by their nature.

Think about what makes one time distinguishable from another. Times are distinguishable by what happens at those times. For example, today you are reading these words, while yesterday you were not (I assume). These different events make up different times. The distinguishability in events, then, explains the distinguishability in times. The point here is that nothing about a time *in itself* makes a difference with respect to which events are possible. An event in which a castle appears on your head has no better chance of happening next week than this week.

We can see that differences in time are irrelevant by the light of reason. By the light of reason, we can see that if a castle cannot appear from nothing today, then a castle cannot appear from nothing at any other time. It *follows* that a castle cannot appear from nothing at the first moment of time. Again, all times are *intrinsically alike*.

Moreover, by the light of reason, we can discover—with some concentration and effort—the *root* of the causal order. The root of the causal order is in the relationship between the *actual* and the *potential*. A mere potential (like Gumby) is not the same as an *actual* something (like some Play-Doh). A mere potential has to be *made* actual if it is to *be* actual. An *automatically actual* foundation, by contrast, does not.

We are now ready to put the pieces together to complete this third step. The foundation is not a mere potential. Instead, it is automatically actual. Therefore, by the Principle of Self-Sufficiency, the foundation has a necessary nature (i.e., it cannot not exist). That means the foundation has no potential to come

Step Four: Eternal

into existence or cease to exist. In other words, the foundation is *eternal*.

This result tells us something about the foundation's current existence. The foundation exists *today*. It didn't stop existing billions of years ago. It is still with us even now.

Notice that this result—that the foundation is eternal—is fully compatible with an *infinite regresss* of prior causes. Some people imagine that the universe has always existed via an infinite sequence of causes. I have not ruled that out. If the universe has always existed, it has always had a foundation—a fundamental layer. If, instead, the universe had a beginning, the result is the same: the foundation of existence is eternal. In other words, whether or not the universe has a beginning or end, the foundation of existence has no beginning or end.

After all of this, you might wonder: how could something exist without any beginning or end? Consider two options. One option is that the foundation exists for an *infinite extent of time*, without a first or last moment. Here is the other: the foundation exists *outside of time* altogether. In either case, the foundation never comes into being or goes out of being. (A third idea is to mix these: the foundation exists outside of time *just if there is no time*; once time exists, the foundation exists in time without ever *coming into being*.)

In summary, the foundation of existence has a stable nature. It cannot be a *mere potential*: mere potentials can be created, while the foundation cannot be created. Therefore, the foundation never was a mere potential; it is *automatically actual*. In other words, the foundation has eternal existence.

STEP FIVE
-PURELY ACTUAL-

We are now ready for the next step. This step will be quite abstract. But you can handle it.

We can use the light of reason to see deeper into the nature of the foundation. Last time, we saw that the foundation is *automatically actual*. That is to say, it has no potential not to exist. In this step, we will draw out a further implication of being automatically actual.

We are now beginning to probe the foundation's *essence*. By "essence," I mean the attributes that comprise its inalterable nature. These are the attributes it cannot *not* have. In other words, it *must*—by its nature—have its essential attributes (the attributes that comprise its essence). My goal is to provide a deeper understanding of the essence of the foundation.

To help us, I will again use the Play-Doh analogy. Imagine some Play-Doh is automatically actual. This Play-Doh, let's say, is the foundation of everything. We can see that certain attributes are *not* part of its essence. For example, being in the form of Gumby is not part of its essence, for the Play-Doh can exist without ever forming Gumby. More generally, no particular shape is part of the essence of the Play-Doh. The Play-Doh's essence is automatically actual, yet no shape is automatically actual.

Reason reveals why no shape is automatically actual. Here is why: shapes differ in merely quantitative ways (e.g., in their number of vertices and size of interior angles), yet mere quantitative differences are not differences in *essence*. Bear with me here. Consider prime numbers. No prime number has the essence of a prime *minister*. The size of the number makes no difference: prime numbers differ from one another merely *quantitatively*, while a prime minister differs from a prime number in a much deeper way. Prime ministers have a different essence. That's why we can be sure that no prime *number*, no matter its magnitude, is a prime *minister*. We don't have to check every prime number or every prime minister to know this. Reason itself makes it clear. In the same way, we can know that no shape (or shapes) can be foundational. The foundation has a deeply different essence.

This observation about shapes may seem abstract and maybe even uninteresting. However, what's at stake is something farther reaching. It's about the essence of the foundation: the foundation's essence lacks *all potentiality*. It lacks the potential to *be* Gumby, since Gumby is a mere potential. Shapes are just one example. The principle behind this example is bigger.

We can state the principle this way: *the foundation is purely actual*. Here is what I mean. The foundation cannot increase or decrease in any essential feature. The foundation is complete in itself. The foundation's *existence* is not the only thing that is automatically actual. So is every essential feature of the foundation. They are also automatically actual.

To draw this out, consider one more example. Let's say the foundation has some powers within its essence, such as the power to produce dependent things. These powers cannot increase or decrease. Instead, the foundation has within its essence all the powers it *could* have within its essence. Its essential powers are automatically actual.

The full significance of this step will come into view as we continue, especially at the end. The next four steps are about specific powers contained within the foundation's essence. Beyond those steps, we will reach the final step, which is about a *root feature* that will explain all other features and powers of the foundation. The step currently beneath our feet will help us reach these later steps, as we shall see.

STEP SIX
-FOUNDATION OF MIND-

We can learn more about the foundation by considering its effects. The next four steps are about the effects of the foundation. Consider some of the foundation's effects: your mind, your body, moral concepts and experiences, and reasoning itself. These effects tell us something about their ultimate cause.

In this section, we will focus on minds. The foundation of *all* that exists is the foundation of *minds*, since minds exist. That's the whole step. The foundation of the world is the foundation of minds. Simple, right?

What is not so simple is seeing *how* anything can be a foundation of minds. How can any mind emerge, ever?

Consider, first, what a mind is. You have a mind. You can think, feel, and form intentions. A mind is anything that is capable of thinking, feeling, and intending to do things.

To help us appreciate the nature of minds, we must distinguish a *genuine* mind from a mere *simulation*. A computer can simulate a mind without having a mind. Imagine, for example, a robot programmed to *act* like it thinks, feels, and intends to do things. It *acts* as if it has a mind, but that doesn't mean it *actually* thinks, feels, or intends anything.

To draw out this point, imagine we make a robot that says, "ouch" if you touch it. Does it thereby *feel* pain? Clearly not. A computer could act like it feels pain without feeling anything.

If there is any doubt, try this. Say "ouch" whenever you feel *happy*. Then you'll confirm that simulating pain is not the same as actually feeling pain.

By seeing the difference between simulating an experience and actually having an experience, you are ready to appreciate one of the toughest questions human beings have ever conceived. It is about *constructing* a mind, an actual mind. How do you do that?

The problem of constructing an actual mind is a hard problem. In fact, philosophers have a name for it. We call it the *Hard Problem*.

The heart of the problem is that some materials are the wrong ingredients for constructing a mind. Just as you cannot construct a chocolate cake out of glass, you cannot construct a mind out of just anything. You need the right materials.

Recall that a construction error results when constructing something out of the wrong materials. For example, we cannot construct a black steel floor out of white marble tiles. Doing so commits a construction error. Likewise, building a mind out of the wrong materials commits a construction error.

Which materials are the wrong materials? Here are some examples. No matter how much funding you have, you will never construct a mind out of *numbers*. Numbers have no power to produce thoughts, feelings, or intentions.

Notice that the problem has nothing to do with complexity. You'll have no better luck constructing a mind out of a large number, like 1,209,381,238, than out of smaller numbers. The problem is not with complexity or size. It is with *category*. Numbers are the wrong category for making a mind.

Similarly, you cannot construct a mind merely by changing the *motions* of things. Suppose you have some sand in your hand. You can throw the sand into the air, but their *motion* is not the same as an *emotion*. No matter how much funding you have, you will never construct an emotion merely by moving things. Mere motion is not enough.

At this point, you might wonder whether science provides the answer. After all, neuroscience reveals that matter does produce minds *somehow*. Thus, if we want to construct a mind, we just need to organize matter into a brain. Problem solved.

However, the problem is much deeper than copying a brain (as if copying a brain were not hard enough!). The deeper problem is to see how any consciousness can exist *in the first place*. While the motions of molecules within a brain affect consciousness, that's only so when someone *capable of consciousness* has that brain. Where did the original conscious capacity come from?

Keep in mind that neuroscience only reveals *correlations*. For example, we see that when axons fire in a certain way, someone reports certain experiences. Mere correlation, however, does nothing to explain how experiences can exist *in the first place*.

Consider the correlation between a light switch and a light bulb. When you flip a light switch, a lamp glows. The flip of the switch is correlated with the glow of the lamp. Yet the correlation does nothing to explain *how* a light switch makes a lamp glow. Why does the lamp glow when you flip a switch?

The problem with consciousness is even deeper. Molecular motions may *simulate* "thoughts," "feelings," or "intentions." But how can any such simulation *be* genuine thoughts, feelings, or intentions? Correlation doesn't answer that. Correlation only labels the mystery.

Once you see this mystery clearly, you can appreciate why some philosophers have denied the existence of minds altogether. I met a philosopher who told me frankly that he didn't think *he* existed. He explained to me that he didn't see how mere particles could—in principle—produce persons. Persons have thoughts, feelings, and intentions. Yet, particles don't have any of those features. He inferred, then, that no persons exist at all.

While skepticism of your own existence may seem odd, I can appreciate how my philosopher friend came to that conclusion. Particles alone do indeed seem to be the wrong materials to produce a conscious being. Packs of particles are just packs of particles. Just as you cannot construct a black steel floor by combining white marble tiles (of any size and arrangement), it is hard to see how you could construct an emotional person, say, merely by combining emotionless particles.

Yet, people do exist. You exist. You can know this by direct awareness of *your* thoughts and feelings. In fact, all knowledge flows ultimately from direct awareness of your experiences. Your knowledge of science flows through your *senses*, of which you are directly aware. If you cannot be aware of your own senses, you cannot be aware of anything.

So I do not recommend the thought that your thoughts don't exist.

I wish to highlight, however, that philosophers who deny the existence of thoughts illustrate a point I made earlier. They illustrate that reasonable people can be blocked from seeing something that *can* be seen. You can see that you have thoughts. Have a thought. See it in your own mind. Notice that you do not posit your thought as the best explanation of your behavior. Rather, you can see your thought *directly*, just by having it.

Yet, my philosopher friend, who denied the sight of his own thoughts, was a reasonable man. His theory of the world blocked his sight. He thought he saw clearly that the foundation lacks the resources to construct any genuinely thinking and feeling beings. This thought blocked him from seeing clearly that *he* is real.

My conversation with the philosopher who denied his own existence was one of the most interesting conversations I have ever had. Over dinner, I proceeded to challenge his assumptions about the foundation of reality. He assumed the foundation was fundamentally *material* (i.e., packs of particles). He argued that non-sensing particles are the wrong materials for constructing persons. I agreed with that part of the argument. However, instead of denying the existence of persons, I wanted him to reassess his understanding of the foundation. Maybe particles *aren't* the most fundamental reality.

On the other hand, for the sake of modesty, I will leave this matter open. I shall leave open precisely what materials are required to construct a mind.

What I say here is just this: the foundation has the right materials, whatever they are, to construct minds. It must. Minds in fact exist. Your mind exists. Therefore, the foundation has the resources to construct a world with your mind in it.

This result implies something about the *essence* of the foundation. The foundation's power to produce possible effects, such as minds, *is part of its essence*. To see this, suppose the foundation had no power. Then in order for the foundation to gain any power, it would need to produce power within itself. Yet, it takes power to produce power. In other words, the foundation cannot produce power without *already having power*. Therefore, the foundation's power is automatically actual. It's part of its essence.

Similarly, the foundation's specific *power to produce minds* (through some chain of causes and effects) is also part of its essence. If the foundation couldn't produce minds, it couldn't gain that power without giving itself that power, since it is the foundation of all powers. Yet, the foundation couldn't give itself the power to produce minds without already having that power. Hence, the power to produce minds is automatically actual. It's part of the foundation's essence.

STEP SEVEN
-FOUNDATION OF MATTER-

If this book were an apologetic for a cosmic designer, I would bring up two scientific discoveries. First, I would talk about the discovery of the Big Bang, which marks a beginning of the cosmos as we know it. Second, I would talk about the discovery of the fine-tuning of the cosmos for complex creatures. These two discoveries are part of a case for a cosmic designer, who fashioned the laws and parameters of our universe.

I won't develop that case here, however. I have a far more ambitious goal. My goal is to give you clear sight of an unsurpassably great treasure. The scientific case is not good enough, for science is based on testimony and probability estimates. But testimony and probability do not reveal perfectly clear sight. They are fallible.

I want each step in our bridge to be based on clear sight. I want you to be able to see each step as clearly as you can see

The Bridge of Reason

your own thoughts. I don't want you to have to trust anyone's word. I don't want you to have to hope that the odds are in your favor. I want your steps to be secure. I want you to have knowledge.

The next step, then, is about something more basic. It is about the foundation's ability to be a foundation of matter, assuming matter exists at all. The step is simple: the foundation of all things is the foundation of all material forms (if there are any). (I don't want to take for granted even that matter exists because I don't want to take anything for granted.)

To help you appreciate *how* a foundation could be a foundation of matter, I will sketch a theory. I do not insist that this theory is correct (though I am inclined to think it is). This theory is not part of the bridge of reason. My purpose here is only to illustrate how the foundation could conceivably produce material forms.

I call my theory, the Imagination Theory. On this theory, the foundation of the world has a power you have: it has the power of imagination. It can produce material forms by *imagining them*. Just as you can form an image of a horse, say, in your mind, the foundation can form particles by imagining them. While your imagination is private to your own mind, the imagination of the foundation is public to all minds. It is *real* in the fullest sense.

This view may seem striking, especially if you are accustomed to thinking of "reality" as ultimately based on mindlessness. I totally understand. I only invite you to entertain the possibility.

The Imagination Theory provides the resources for explaining both material forms and physical laws. Physical laws reflect *rational thoughts* in the mind of the foundation. For example, the law that "dense" material forms attract in a certain way is based on the *thought* that they attract in that way. The law has the same structure as the thought: both "say" that things of a certain type do certain things under certain conditions. Laws have the structure of a thought because laws *are* thoughts. More precisely, laws are thoughts *acted upon*.

This "thoughts" account of laws can explain the psycho-physical laws that hold between your own thoughts and chemical reactions in your brain. For example, positive thoughts can affect the physical health of your brain because there is a law that certain axons in your brain fire in a certain way when you have certain thoughts. This law is the (acted upon) *thought* that certain axons fire in a certain way when you have certain thoughts.

These laws provide an orderly world. The foundation can maintain an orderly world by its rational thoughts. In this way, the foundation can produce a world in which complex creatures with minds live and move and have their being.

According to the Imagination Theory, matter is organized by the imagination and thoughts of a rational, orderly mind. This theory explains why matter never vanishes like vapor or scatters randomly. A rational foundation provides a foundation for order throughout the universe. It provides a foundation for science.

Whether you accept the Imagination Theory or not, the conclusion so far is this: the foundation of all that exists is the foundation of the material world (if it exists).

STEP EIGHT
-FOUNDATION OF MORALS-

Let us review our steps. We began with the universal observation that something exists. From there, we saw a puzzle about existence: why does anything exist? This puzzle is about how reality, in total, can be *uncreated*, despite everything else being *created*. How can that be? We found a solution: reality, in total, is uncreated because the foundation of reality is uncreated. We then began to explore the nature of the foundation.

By reason and reflection, we deduced the following features of the foundation: the foundation is (i) self-sufficient (not created), (ii) automatically actual (i.e., without the potential not to be actual), (iii) eternal, (iv) purely actual (i.e., without the potential to increase or decrease in its essential features), (v) foundational to all minds, and (vi) foundational to all matter (if there is matter).

We will now consider another feature of the foundation. The foundation has, within its essence, the power to produce a world with moral agents.

What is a moral agent? Let's take an example: *you.* You are a moral agent. Here is what I mean by that. You have moral concepts, like right and wrong, good and bad. You also have moral sensations, like remorse, vindication, or a sense of obligation to tell the truth. Moral agents have moral concepts and moral sensations. They are able to discern right from wrong.

Moral concepts and moral sensations are as familiar as air, but they are not trivial. We can easily imagine a world without any moral agents. For example, imagine that evolution spawns an army of amoral machines. Since these machines are not moral agents, they lack moral concepts and moral sensations. We could imagine that these machines somehow gain consciousness. For example, let's say the machines can feel hot and cold. Still, feeling hot or cold is not the same as sensing right or wrong. The existence of consciousness does not ensure the existence of moral agents.

The relationship between consciousness and moral sensation is like the relationship between being colorful and having a specific color, like pink. Just as something can be colorful without being pink, something could have consciousness without having any moral sensations at all.

Could the mechanisms of evolution, like natural selection, explain how moral properties emerged? It is not clear how. Natural selection selects from what exists. Yet we can easily imagine a world in which every aggregate of molecules lacks every moral sensation. Survival of the fittest doesn't explain how moral sensations can arise in the first place.

We have a construction problem. Just as there is a Hard Problem of constructing consciousness from non-consciousness, there is also a hard problem of constructing moral sensations from non-moral molecules. How is that even possible?

Consider the *sense* of goodness. What is that sense composed of? Could you construct the sense of goodness from ice-cubes? From leaves on a tree? From sand?

Recall that some constructions commit a construction error. You cannot construct black steel from white marble. Similarly, you cannot construct the feeling of sadness from sand. To construct those things from those materials is to commit a construction error. In the same way, to construct the feeling of goodness from a bag of candies is to commit a construction error.

The obvious question, then, is this: how do you construct a moral agent?

You may have noticed that I have not said anything about whether morality is *objective*. I have decided not to enter the objective vs. subjective debate here, for I do not want us to get distracted away from a more basic observation. You have moral concepts and sensations. That is significant.

We can debate whether any of your moral concepts reflect objective features of reality. For example, we can debate whether your moral concept of the wrongness of murder tracks with a moral reality that exists independently of you. (Was murder wrong before you were born?) Regardless, you *have* moral concepts and sensations. For example, you have the concept of murder being wrong. The mere existence of moral concepts is significant enough for our purposes.

Return to the question at hand: how can moral agents emerge? Suppose particles compose the fundamental layer of reality. How do those particles produce moral sensations, like courage, compassion, or the feeling of purpose? *Can* they? Can particles produce the sense that truth-seeking is more noble than false-hood seeking? How?

Perhaps we can wave the wand of "evolution." By evolution, particles produce people. By evolution, molecules make minds. By evolution, the feeling of right and wrong is bound to emerge.

However, evolution doesn't solve the construction problem. Evolution can do powerful things with the ingredients it has. But the deeper question—the question for those who want penetrating insight—is about the *ingredients*. What kind of a foundation has the ingredients to produce the kind of beings who can ask this very question? What kind of ingredients can produce a moral agent like *you*?

It is tempting to translate tough questions into something easier. The Pythagoreans wanted to analyze everything in terms of *numbers* because they liked numbers and understood them. These days, the temptation is to analyze everything in terms of *shapes*, or other "material" properties we think we understand.

Hard questions are hard. It would be easier if we could translate them into something else. That's understandable. It is reasonable. But it does not lead to insight. The path to insight is to face the "hard" reality. Otherwise, we only change the subject.

For the sake of modesty, I will leave open the precise answer to the question at hand (at least for now). Instead, I will make an obvious deduction, a deduction you can *know* is true once you see it. The deduction proceeds as follows. The ultimate foundation, by definition, is the ultimate foundation of all effects. Moral agents are among the effects. They exist, after all. Therefore, the ultimate foundation is the ultimate foundation of moral agents.

Somehow, then, the foundation has the right ingredients to produce moral concepts and moral sensations. These ingredients give the foundation the power to produce a world in which moral beings, like you, can exist.

I will call a foundation that has the power to produce moral agents 'a moral foundation'. The foundation of existence, then, is a moral foundation. It has the power—the ingredients—to produce the sense of good as well as the concept of departing from goodness.

Before I conclude this section, I will paint a fuller picture of the moral foundation. This picture is not essential to our bridge of reason. I offer it for the sake of illustration. The picture illustrates the resourcefulness of a moral foundation.

I offer, then, a theory of how the moral foundation—something with the ingredients to produce moral agents—can explain morality. To start, a moral foundation can contain the ultimate Standards of Goodness within its *essence*. For example, let us say that murder is wrong because murder breaks a principle of love. We might state the principle this way: moral agents should love one another. This principle of love is part of the Standard of Goodness, which is part of the essence of the moral foundation.

This theory bears fruit. By anchoring moral principles in the essence of the foundation, we can explain why certain moral principles seem to be *unalterable*. For example, the principle that moral agents, if there are moral agents, should love one another is like the principle that $2 + 2 = 4$. While our *knowledge* of these principles is variable, the principles themselves are unalterable. Harming people just for the sake of harming them is not okay on Tuesdays, or at any other time.

Another fruit of this theory is that it side-steps a famous concern about grounding morality in a divine agent. The concern targets the theory that morality comes entirely from God's *will*. The concern is this. Suppose all morality comes from God's will. Then morality is arbitrary. Murder would only be bad because God says it is bad. Yet that contradicts intuition: it seems murder is bad *just because it harms people*. It is bad to harm people, regardless of what anyone, even a god, says or thinks. Do you agree?

If you do agree, then you might appreciate an irony that many people miss. Many moral skeptics are sympathetic with the intuition that a god cannot make murder okay just by commanding us to murder people. Yet, this very intuition underwrites *objective* morality. For objective morality just is the set of principles and values that hold independently of what anyone (even a god) happens to say or think.

To be clear, my purpose is not to insist on the objectivity of morality. My purpose, rather, is to show the resourcefulness of a moral foundation. A moral foundation could anchor principles of love, justice, and goodness within its essence. These principles would then be "automatically actual" because the foundation's essence is automatically actual. The foundation, then, has the right resources for an objective moral order. It has the right nature.

A moral foundation has even more resources. A moral foundation contains the *reason* for the existence of moral agents. Let me explain. Abstract principles, by themselves, comprise only one dimension of a moral landscape. There is another dimension. The other dimension is the dimension of moral subjects—beings, like you, *who can understand moral principles*. For example, you can understand the principle that moral agents should love each other. This love *principle* is not the same as a *person* who can live by the love principle.

Moral agents are not automatically given. We could conceive of a world in which there are moral principles without any moral agents to appreciate them. For example, the following principle could be true: *if* moral agents exist, *then* they should love each other. That *if-then* principle could be true *whether or not* any moral agents exist at all.

Why would a moral foundation produce a world with beings like you in it? Here is a hypothesis: you are valuable. This hypothesis follows from a more general moral principle: all moral agents have *intrinsic value*—i.e., value by virtue of the kind of thing it is. You are a moral agent—a being with moral concepts and sensations. Hence, you have intrinsic value. Your value, then, is a *reason* for the moral foundation to produce a world with you in it.

This account implies that the moral foundation is able to act on reasons. The foundation is able to "see" that you are valuable and then act on this sight. This sight gives it the power to design a world in which beings like you emerge.

I realize that you might question whether the foundation has the power to "see" anything. I anticipate that. It is good to question everything. I do not want us to step along our bridge too quickly. At this place on the bridge, you do not need to agree with my more specific theory of the moral foundation. I offer it for your consideration, but we can continue our journey without it.

Our journey requires just this step: the foundation of everything is the foundation of moral agents. That is to say, the foundation has, within its essence, the power to create a world with beings who can sense right and wrong, good and bad. The foundation has the right resources.

In summary, we can learn about a cause from its effects. Moral agents, like you, are among the effects. Therefore, the foundation of all effects has the power to produce moral agents. In other words, the foundation of existence is the foundation of morals.

STEP NINE
-FOUNDATION OF MATH-

This next step is about something few people on earth have thought much about. Don't get me wrong. *Some* people have thought much about what's coming. But not many. This next step is about the foundation of mathematics and logic.

What is math? What is logic? Within your mind, you can witness principles of mathematics and logic. For example, you can witness that 2 + 2 = 4. You can witness that whatever is true is not also false. You can witness that A is A, for any A. What are these principles, and why do they exist at all?

Let us not make the mistake of conflating the obvious with the trivial. Principles of math and logic may be obvious, but they are far from trivial.

At first glance, we might be tempted to think that principles, like 2 + 2 = 4, are no more (or less) significant than the existence of *thoughts*. In fact, we might think these principles *just are* our thoughts. For example, 2 + 2 = 4 is our thought about some numbers.

However, on closer inspection, we can see that there must be more to math than our thoughts. Our thoughts can be mistaken, after all. For the sake of focus, consider *your* thoughts. Have you ever made a mistake adding up numbers? You could *think* that 2,017 + 3,023 = 5,030. If you did, your thought would be a mistake. 2,017 + 3,023 is *not* 5,030; it's 5,040. By inference, then, your mathematical thoughts are not automatically *correct* mathematical thoughts. In the same way, *groups* of people can make mathematical mistakes. For example, you and I could both make the same mistake. It is even conceivable that *everyone* makes the same mistake. Imagine that everyone accidentally thinks that 2,017 apples plus 3,023 apples = 5,030 apples. What would that imply? It would imply we were all wrong.

The reason I am drawing attention to the possibility of everyone being wrong is to make clear that "correct" thoughts are not the same as *universally-held* ones. A mathematical belief could be universally-held but still wrong.

What, then, makes a mathematical thought *correct*? This question is an instance of a general question: what makes *any* thought correct? The answer is this: a thought is *correct* if it matches actual reality. For example, your thought that you have eyes is correct if you actually have eyes—i.e., your eyes are part of actual reality. Similarly, the thought that 2 + 2 = 4 is correct if 2 + 2 actually equals 4. In other words, mathematical thoughts are correct if they match a mathematical reality.

Let me reassure you. I am well aware that intelligent people debate the nature of mathematical reality. If you worry that I am going too far or too fast, let me be clear: I am not going to attempt to resolve every debate about the nature of mathematics. That's way too much to do. It is not necessary for our purposes.

Instead, here I wish only to draw your attention to the reality of at least certain principles of mathematics and logic, putting aside questions about their nature. The principle that 2 + 2 = 4 is real. So is the principle that if A exists, then A exists. These principles are part of the real world, perhaps an "abstract" part of the world.

Principles of mathematics and logic are what I call *reason*. Reason consists of all the correct principles of mathematics and logic. As before, we can distinguish between your thinking and correct thinking. While your thinking can be correct, it is not automatically correct. Your thinking can fall off the rails of correct reasoning.

It is now time to state the obvious: the foundation of everything is the foundation of correct reasoning. That's the ninth step.

Here is how the foundation can be a foundation of correct reasoning. Just as we can theorize that the foundation includes the moral principles within its essence, we can also theorize that the foundation includes the principles of correct reasoning within its essence. On this account, the foundation is both the Standard of Good and the Standard of Reason. Goodness and Reason exist in the essence of the foundation. I will call a foundation with reason in its essence 'a rational foundation'.

A rational foundation makes sense of how there can be any principles of reason at all. Reason is about how thinkers should think. It is about correct thinking. Why should reality care to include principles about how *thinkers* should think? (That makes it sound like reality cares about us!) A rational foundation explains why there are principles of reason within reality. There are principles of reason within reality because a rational foundation includes reason within its essence

A rational foundation also has the resources to produce *thinkers*. Just as a *moral* foundation has resources to produce moral agents, a *rational* foundation has resources to produce agents who can think. Here is how. The rational foundation includes the following reasoning: *if thinkers are valuable beings, then it is good for thinkers to exist.* The *moral* principle that thinkers are valuable provides the rational foundation with a *reason* to produce thinkers. This reason can then help explain why the foundation has in fact produced a world in which thinkers have emerged.

Inspired by modesty, however, I do not want to insist that my account of a rational foundation is correct. What I want you to see for now is (*at least*) this much: the foundation of everything is the foundation of the rational dimension of reality.

That means the foundation has, within its essence, the right resources for producing a world with thinkers who can apprehend that (say) 2 + 2 = 4. In short, the foundation of all existence is also the foundation of reason.

STEP TEN
-THE GREATEST TREASURE-

It is now time for the most exciting step. It is about the greatest conceivable treasure.

Let us retrace our steps up to this point. We began by recognizing that *something* exists. That was the first step. From there, we began seeking an understanding of the *foundation* of existence. We uncovered eight features from two directions. First, we looked *into* the foundation with the light of reason. We deduced four features: the foundation is (i) self-sufficient (not created), (ii) automatically actual (i.e., without the potential not to be actual), (iii) eternal, and (iv) purely actual (i.e., without the potential to increase or decrease in its essential features).

Next, we looked *above* the foundation, at its effects. By reflecting on the effects, we inferred four more features: the foundation is (v) foundational to all minds, (vi) foundational to all matter (if there is matter), (vii) foundational to morals, and

(viii) foundational to reason itself.

We are now ready to look *even deeper into* the foundation. We are ready to uncover a feature that explains every other feature of the foundation.

Before I proceed, I want to highlight the value of explaining features. An explanation of diverse features illuminates the nature of those features. Consider, for example, the diverse features of biological creatures. Rabbits, fish, and plants vary in substantial ways. Yet, they share a common feature: they all have DNA. This common feature within each living creature points to a common origin. The shared feature of DNA implies that diverse creatures sprang from a common root. By understanding this common feature, we illuminate the nature of the biological world.

To further illustrate the value of an explanation, let us take another example. Physicists seek to understand the physical world by discovering physical laws, like gravity and electromagnetism. But they are also seeking a more basic law that can explain all the others. Why are they doing that? Why do they search for a basic, unifying law? Here is one reason: a basic law that explains the others would illuminate the others. It would give us a deeper understanding of the entire physical world. An explanation of diverse things illuminates those things.

One more example. Let's say you discover a letter next to some flowers. This letter has your name on it. As you read the letter, you read the following words, "I just wanted you to know that I love you. You are special." At this point, you might form the hypothesis that this letter was written by someone who loves you. This hypothesis would explain the letter. It would *also* explain why there are flowers next to the letter. Your single hypothesis illuminates your diverse observations.

In the same way, a deeper explanation of the features of the foundation would illuminate those diverse features. Let us consider, then, what might explain the foundation's features.

I don't want us to guess. I want us to *see*. Let us take the light of reason in hand and see what we can see.

By reason, we can see something that all eight features we've identified have in common. All eight features point to a more basic feature. They point to a *supreme nature*.

Allow me to explain. Imagine you want to write someone a love letter. You tell them they are special. You then begin to list some reasons you think they are special. Here are some things you might say: you are kind; you are intelligent; you are talented. These features have something in common: they are all *positive*. By contrast, you would not say this: you are *evil*. Intuitively, being evil is not a positive feature.

While I wish to be as ecumenical as possible, at this step, I will need to carve a crucial distinction. I need to separate *genuinely positive* features from *merely liked* features. They aren't the same. For example, if someone is being reasonable, their reasonableness is a positive feature. This feature is positive even if they happen not to *like* being reasonable.

Regardless of their likes, it is still good to be reasonable; it is still positive.

Similarly, suppose everyone hates you. That doesn't mean you have no positive features. You have the positive feature of *being valuable*. Your value does not depend on what people think of you. It doesn't even depend on what *you* think of you. You have value because of the kind of being you are—a person.

I am well aware that we have come upon a stumbling block. Many people insist that all "value" is purely in the eye of the beholder. Truth, beauty, and goodness are "valuable" only by being liked. Hence, if nothing were liked, nothing would have value. Not even you.

I am torn. On the one hand, I think it is possible to clearly separate positive features from merely liked features. On the other, I realize that vapors of subjectivism have seeped deeply into some sectors of society. If you happen to be convinced that all value is subjective, I am not sure I will be able to change your mind about that. At least not easily, not here. In any case, I don't want to *have to* change your mind.

So, I have decided to try something else. I will propose a translation. When I talk of "positive features," you may translate the term "positive" in terms of what you could rationally value—esteem, praise, or desire—*for its own sake*. For example, wisdom is positive because you can value wisdom for its own sake. Pain, by contrast, is not positive, because the only reason anyone could desire or value pain is for the sake of something *else*, like to accomplish a task, or to feel alive.

By understanding a "positive" feature as intrinsically valuable (i.e., what you can value for its own sake), I hope we can move past this stumbling block.

Perhaps you will feel some reassurance by seeing how the translation can make sense of *likes* and *dislikes*. For example, let us say you like vanilla ice cream. We can explain that: you tend to have a certain positive taste experience when you eat vanilla ice cream. This positive taste experience is itself desirable. Your desire for vanilla, then, is *for the sake of a positive experience*. Meanwhile, your friend might prefer chocolate ice cream. The reason they prefer it, though, is for the same reason you prefer vanilla—to have an intrinsically desirable experience. The positive experience, while caused in different ways, is itself desirable *for its own sake*.

As a final note about positive features, I would like to draw attention to a certain irony in denying the existence of positive features. The irony is about motivation. Suppose someone denies the existence of all positive features. In that case, they've denied the *value* of making that very denial. Why make it then? What could be their motivation? Implicit in their motivation is desire (i.e., the desire to assert something true). And implicit in their desire is an *end* desire (i.e., the desire to feel vindicated or understood)—that which they value for its own sake. You see the irony: for them to deny that anything is valuable as an end (i.e., valuable for its own sake) is to reveal their interest *in some*

The Bridge of Reason

end (i.e., in something that is valuable for its own sake). Their very assertion contradicts their own motivation

In a sense, then, denying all value is self-defeating. Just as doubting the existence of everything reveals the existence of your doubt, denying the value of everything reveals the value of your denial.

I hope I have said enough to orient you to the concept of "positive" I have in mind.

Return now to our inquiry. We are seeking an explanation of the features of the foundation. Recall our catalogue of features: the foundation is (i) self-sufficient, (ii) automatically actual, (iii) eternal, (iv) purely actual, (v) foundational to all minds, (vi) foundational to all matter (if there is matter), (vii) foundational to morals, and (viii) foundational to reason itself. Is there anything that unifies these features? Yes. All these features are predicted if the foundation has *supreme value*.

Suppose, for sake of hypothesis, that the foundation has supreme value. This hypothesis has great explanatory power. To see its power, consider what a supreme (i.e., maximally valuable) foundation would be like. Intuitively, it would be *perfect* in every positive respect. (It would have features that are desirable for their own sake.)

A supreme foundation would have all eight features we have seen. First, it would be self-sufficient—i.e., it would have a supreme ability to exist on its own. Next, it would be automatically actual. That's because valuable things are more valuable if they maintain their value. If you have a valuable thing, like a diamond ring, its value is enhanced if its value cannot be easily diminished or destroyed. The most valuable thing, then, would have the most stable value. Third, and for the same reason, a supreme foundation would have eternal value. Fourth, the value of a supreme foundation would be part of its essence (i.e., it would be purely actual along every positive feature).

Additionally, a supreme foundation would have the features that explain the four *effects* we considered. First, a truly supreme foundation would have a supreme mind (because there is more value in having knowledge than in lacking knowledge), giving it the intellectual capacity to produce all minds. Second, a supreme foundation would have supreme power, from which it could produce every material configuration. Third, a supreme foundation would have supreme moral virtue. This virtue, together with its supreme mind, would explain why it contains the resources to produce moral agents. Fourth, and finally, a supreme foundation would, by virtue of its supreme mind, contain perfect reasoning. Its perfect reasoning in turn explains the reality of reason itself: reason exists because the foundation is supremely reasonable.

What I am trying to convey to you is how a supreme nature *unifies* all the features of the foundation. A supreme nature predicts every feature we have identified. It *explains* every feature. In this way, a supreme nature illuminates the entire

The Bridge of Reason

nature of the foundation.

By illuminating the foundation of everything, we also illuminate everything "above" the foundation. Consider, again, that beings like you exist. You (and beings like you) anchor together an array of fascinating features: you have a material form (I assume), as well as thoughts, sensations, and moral concepts. Plus, you have sight of principles of reason. Why are there such beings as you? A supreme foundation illuminates why. Just as value underwrites the features of the foundation, value underwrites your features. *You* are a valuable being. A supreme foundation would see your value and thus have reason to fashion a world for your eventual existence.

Let us have a closer look at this final step. I want to release to you *knowledge*, not a mere guess. I am not content even to give you the best explanation. Maybe a supreme nature is a supreme explanation. But is it the *correct* explanation? Is there any way to know for sure?

I think there is. Follow this path. By reason, we can see that if the foundation has any valuable features, then the foundation has some value. How much? We might wonder, for the sake of simplicity, whether the foundation has *no* value. Yet, the foundation has many valuable features, such as *uniqueness*, *maximally-robust existence*, and *the ability to produce all value*. By reason, we know that the foundation cannot simultaneously *have value* and *have no value*. Hence, since the foundation has *some* value (by its valuable features), we can rule out the hypothesis that it has *no* value. So, again, we can ask how much value it has. Here is the next simplest answer: the foundation has *all*—or *supreme*—value. Could that be right?

We need not speculate. We can see the answer clearly through the lens of *pure actuality*.

Recall the step about pure actuality. It was an abstract step. When I introduced that step, its value was hard to discern. But we are now ready to appreciate its full value. You see, the foundation has a purely actual essence that contains *at least some* value. It contains at least some value because of its valuable features. But if it contains at least some value, then by virtue of its pure actuality, it must have value *through and through*. Its value must be complete—and therefore supreme.

To draw out this step, consider again what it means to be purely actual. The foundation is purely actual because its essential features are *automatically actual*. And whatever is automatically actual cannot be a mere potential. Limits, by contrast, are not automatically actual. Every limit of an object marks a boundary between the actual and the merely potential. A tree that is limited in its size, for example, has a size that marks a boundary between its actual size and a potential size. Of the increase in *potential* limit, there is no end. (Even limited abstract things, like numbers, go up indefinitely, without end.) The *purely actual* foundation, then, cannot have any feature within its essence that marks a boundary—a limit—between the actual and the merely potential. Hence, no feature within the essence of the foundation can be limited.

Here is another way to see this same result from another angle. The foundation is the ultimate source of all *actual* as well as all *possible* value, for nothing that could exist could exist apart from the foundation. Only a supremely valuable foundation could be the ultimate source of all possible value. Therefore, the foundation is supremely valuable.

Supreme value not only explains the eight other attributes we have identified, it also provides a tool for investigating other features of the foundation. Every feature of the foundation must be consistent with supreme value. We can deduce, for example, that the foundation is not a flying spaghetti monster, with arbitrary limits. Moreover, we can deduce three more features that flow from supreme value: *supreme knowledge*, *supreme power*, and *moral perfection*. The foundation of existence, then, is the greatest possible Being.

We now arrive at the final step on our bridge: the foundation of existence has supreme value. It is the supreme treasure. It is the treasure that makes all treasures possible. It is the treasure that makes your life possible. It is the treasure at the end of the bridge of reason. This treasure is the existence of God.

NEXT STEPS

My purpose has been to help you see a great treasure. I want you to see this treasure because the sight of it can positively transform your journey in life. It can illuminate the meaning and purpose of the world and everything in it. It can inspire a greater vision of your own worth.

By seeing the treasure at the foundation of existence, you gain power to see the significance of your life. The existence of a supreme foundation implies that you are the product of supreme value. Your existence is not an accident. Your life is not ultimately meaningless. Rather, your life is full of meaning. It is full of value.

I want to suggest to you that your life has more value than you know. Your story has more value than you have estimated. Your life has value that is rooted in the supreme value of the supreme foundation of everything.

My goal, then, is not merely academic. I do not merely seek to uncover a clever truth. Rather, I seek to expose a truth that you may treasure.

People sometimes worry that belief in a treasure, especially a *great* treasure, must be based on wishful-thinking. They say it is too good to be true.

Yet, some truths are good.

Why think the ultimate truths about existence are *not good*? The purpose of the bridge of reason is to help you see, not guess or merely wish, that the foundation is good. It is supreme.

The bridge of reason is for you to test and explore. Test for yourself whether the steps I have laid out are secure. Study the bridge. Examine the steps from many angles. Press against them. See if they break beneath you, or if they gain strength under pressure. Only you can assess how things seem to you.

I have a prediction: the more you test the bridge of reason, the more you will see its strength. Maybe you will discover that a certain interpretation of a step has weaknesses, while another interpretation is solid like diamond. Whatever the case, this much is certain: the more truth you seek, the more you will find.

If you would like to explore this bridge in more depth, I have another, longer book, *How Reason Can Lead to God* (with Intervarsity Press, Academic), where I describe this bridge in far greater detail. I add several additional beams that emerge from advances in logic and analytical philosophy. In that book, I also examine common barriers to belief in a Supreme Being. I address, for example, the problem of pain and suffering, and I offer my analysis of the toughest questions I have wrestled with personally. If you would like to learn more about this in-depth book and other resources for designing your worldview, see the author section at the end of this book for contact details.

I would like to close this book by sharing a vision I have of the future of humankind. I see people from all walks of life exchanging valuable insights, freely and from love. Instead of fighting for a favorite tribe, we are learning from each other. We are discovering things together. Just as diverse people come together to build a city, people from all walks of life come together to build a city of knowledge about the things that matter most. In my vision, people across tribes and cultures begin to see—from a thousand unique angles—two universal truths with increasing clarity: first, all people are immeasurably valuable, and second, the *foundation* of all things is supreme. The knowledge of these truths fills the earth as the waters cover the sea. Rather than spearing people with the truth, people everywhere celebrate the knowledge of good things.

If you resonate with my vision, join me in making it a reality.

ABOUT THE AUTHOR

Joshua L. Rasmussen, Ph.D., is a professor of philosophy at Azusa Pacific University. His work in philosophy centers on the ultimate foundation of things and the nature of thought. He is author of several books, including *Defending the Correspondence Theory of Truth* (Cambridge University Press) and *Necessary Existence*, with A. Pruss (Oxford University).

As of the date of publication of this book, the book, *How Reason Can Lead to God*, is still forthcoming (estimated release date: June 2019). If you would like to be the first to know about its release, feel free to send Rasmussen an e-mail at jrasmus1@gmail.com with the subject "bridge of reason." You will then receive notification when the other book is available.

Rasmussen's philosophical work is not limited to books and articles. He is founder of the Worldview Design YouTube channel, which helps people use reason to address the big questions of life. He is also the producer of interactive tools for exploring surprising ways your otherwise ordinary beliefs may piece together to reveal something about the ultimate foundation of reality. (See, for example, necessarybeing.com.) You can find links to all these resources, as well as others, from Rasmussen's website, joshualrasmussen.com.

Thank you for reading!

www.ingramcontent.com/pod-product-compliance
Lightning Source LLC
Chambersburg PA
CBHW031453040426
42444CB00007B/1087